KENT
A PORTRAIT IN COLOUR

MERESBOROUGH BOOKS

Published by
Meresborough Books,
17 Station Road, Rainham,
Kent. ME8 7RS.

ISBN 0948193 700

© Copyright 1992
Meresborough Books

Printed by T P Print,
Sittingbourne, Kent.
Bound by Hartnolls Ltd,
Bodmin, Cornwall.

INTRODUCTION

This book makes no claim to be either a guide or a definitive history; it is simply a collection of colour photographs, selected to show the rich diversity of scenery and historic places to be found in Kent. For this reason the captions accompanying each view have been kept deliberately short, giving only sufficient information to identify the subject matter. Readers who would like to know more about the county, or about specific places and events, are recommended to consult the wealth of good local history books available.

Kent is still a beautiful county, despite its heavy population and proximity to London. It is hoped this book will whet the appetite of readers wishing to know more, or serve as a reminder of times happily spent exploring the rich tapestry of Kent's heritage.

Most of the photographs in the following pages were taken especially for the book. Except where otherwise indicated (in brackets at the end of the relevant caption) they were taken by John Guy, who has also provided the captions. We hope you will enjoy browsing through this delightful collection of colour photographs.

Above: **Smallhythe Place.** This beautiful 16th century house, owned by the National Trust, was once the home of the actress Dame Ellen Terry.

Front Cover: **Rochester Castle.** A fine view of the 12th century castle, taken from the bridge crossing the River Medway.

Back cover: **Canterbury.** A fascinating view of Canterbury's streets floodlit against the night sky.   (Eric Baldock)

Overleaf: **Smarden.** A delightful village, Smarden boasts a number of timbered cottages and is perhaps the epitome of an English village.

Leeds Castle. Built on two natural islands in the centre of a glassy lake and surrounded by 500 acres of magnificent parkland and gardens, Leeds Castle is England's oldest and most romantic stately home. The Castle is a treasurehouse of fine furnishings, tapestries and paintings, whilst in the grounds visitors are encouraged to visit a maze, secret grotto and exotic aviaries.

(Leeds Castle Enterprises)

Above: **Ramsgate.** Still very much a working port, the harbour at Ramsgate now also bustles with yachts and private craft, attracted by some of the finest marina facilities in the south. The town enjoys a friendly rivalry with neighbouring Margate, the fine sands and excellent facilities of both attracting many summer visitors.

Opposite Top: **Pegwell Bay.** This replica of a Viking ship was sailed across the North Sea by a party of Danes in 1949 to commemorate the 1500th anniversary of the first Viking landings. This wide bay was also the landing place of St Augustine in 597 when he arrived from Rome to convert the pagan English.

Opposite Bottom: **Margate.** The seafront at Margate is one of the most popular in the south-east, boasting a fine sandy beach, 'Dreamland' theme park, amusement arcades and much more besides. In stark contrast to its genteel neighbour, Broadstairs, Margate has often been termed 'the Blackpool of the south'.

Above: **Rochester Cathedral.** The second oldest cathedral in England, Rochester is also one of the smallest. Founded in 604, the present building dates mostly from the Norman period, but with later additions. The magnificent west front (seen here) is particularly ornate.

Left: **Rochester, Dickens' Chalet.** This delightful little building stands in the grounds of Eastgate House, now the Dickens Centre. For many years it stood in the author's garden at Gad's Hill Place, Higham, where he used it as a summer house and writing room. (Mrs V. Harris)

Opposite: **Rochester Castle.** One of the earliest and finest examples of a Norman keep, Rochester is also the tallest at 113ft. The first castle to be built here was in 1080, though only fragments of that structure remain, the mighty keep being added in 1127.

Penshurst. One of the showplaces of Kent, Penshurst is another village of pure delight, where almost every building seems perfect. In this case not all is genuine, for many of the houses were built only about 1850 in picturesque Tudor style. Nearby is the magnificent Penshurst Place, manorial home of the Sidney family.

Tenterden. Considered by many to be one of our finest country towns, Tenterden displays a delightful mix of building styles from medieval to modern. The view above shows the mainly Georgian fronts of the houses and shops that line the lower end of the High Street. The unusually wide street is characteristic of towns where the market was formerly held in the centre of the road.

Above: **Biddenden.** A charming Wealden village with two noteworthy features. In the early twelfth century it was the home of Eliza and Mary Chalkhurst, Siamese twins, who left land to provide food for the poor of the parish. The tradition is still maintained each Easter when special biscuits are doled out. An effigy of the twins appears on the village sign. The second feature is the unique stone pavement, a rare sight in Kent, and clearly seen in this view.

Opposite Top: **Maidstone, the River Medway and Archbishop's Palace.** Alongside the River Medway, in the heart of the town, is this fine collection of medieval buildings. To the left of the view can be seen the Archbishop's Palace, built between 1349 and 1366. To the right of that stands the church, built by Archbishop Courtenay, with the College of Secular Canons beyond. In all, a delightful array of buildings.

(Eric Baldock)

Opposite Bottom: **Maidstone, Tythe Barn.** Originally the stables for the Archbishop's Palace, this magnificent medieval barn houses the Tyrwhitt Drake Museum of Carriages. Inside can be seen a fascinating collection of horse-drawn vehicles from the last 200 years. It also affords a rare opportunity to view the interior of a Kentish barn, so many of which have now been converted into private residences.   (Eric Baldock)

Left: **Chiddingstone.** This tiny village is famed as being one of the most picturesque and unspoilt in the county, the houses displaying both medieval and Tudor features. Nearby can be seen an outcrop of rock known as the *Chiding Stone*, from which the village reputedly takes its name.

Below: **Tonbridge Castle.** The splendid gatehouse of Tonbridge Castle, built about 1276, is one of the finest in Kent, rivalling even those built by Edward I in Wales. The Georgian house to the right of the view was built in 1790-92 and incorporates part of the medieval chapel.

Opposite: **The Pantiles, Tunbridge Wells.** One of the few towns in Kent of relatively recent foundation, Tunbridge Wells is also one of the most elegant. The Pantiles, first built in 1638, still retains some original stone flags, or tiles, from which the area later took its name.

Above: **Deal Seafront.** Deal is unique in Kent in that it is a port without a harbour. Local fishermen take advantage of the steeply shelving shingle banks to beach their craft. Very much a working port, rather than a seaside resort, Deal is a fascinating maritime town, well worth exploring. Just visible to the right of this view is another unusual feature, the pier, constructed of concrete and popular with anglers.

Opposite Top: **Deal Castle.** Framed by trees, lawns and laburnum, time has softened this view of Deal Castle, originally an austere artillery fort rather than a castle proper. Built by Henry VIII between 1538 and 1540, it is one of four such castles constructed in Kent to protect the Downs, a safe harbour for shipping off the Goodwin Sands. Low in stature, the three tiers of defences can be clearly seen here.

Opposite Bottom: **Sandwich, the Barbican Gate and River Stour.** Sandwich is one of the surprises of Kent, displaying one of the finest arrays of medieval buildings in England. The tortuously narrow streets still follow the medieval plan and are a delight to explore on foot. The gatehouse, to the right of the photograph, is the Barbican, one of two gates to survive that once formed part of the town's medieval defences.

Canterbury Cathedral. Without doubt one of the finest medieval cathedrals in Europe, Canterbury is also the oldest in England, founded originally in 597 by St Augustine. Nothing of that first church survives today, but the cathedral shows a wealth of building styles from the Norman period onwards. This view shows the splendid west front, with its twin towers and entrance vestibule, as seen by all visitors entering the precincts by the Christ Church Gate.

Westgate Gardens, Canterbury. In spring and early summer the Westgate Gardens look a picture with the massed plantings of bulbs and bedding plants on the banks of the River Stour. The church in the background is the Holy Cross Church. (Tom Fowler)

Above: **Knole House, Sevenoaks.** Knole is one of the largest private houses in England, standing amidst a vast 1,000 acre deer park. Thomas Bourchier, then Archbishop, started the present mansion in 1456. Elizabeth I later gave it to Sir Thomas Sackville, whose descendants still live in a private wing.

Opposite Top: **Westerham.** The unusual sloping green at Westerham plays host to a statue of one of its greatest residents, Sir Winston Churchill, who lived at nearby Chartwell. Sitting almost astride the borders of both London and Surrey, the village has grown now to the status of small town.

Opposite Bottom: **Chartwell.** Once the home of Sir Winston Churchill, Chartwell is now owned by the National Trust. The house is more interesting than beautiful and was greatly extended by Churchill. A medieval house still stands somewhere inside, submerged beneath later building. (Eric Baldock)

Reculver. The twin towers of Reculver, known as the 'Two Sisters', are virtually all that remain of this early Norman church. Originally founded about 669 and rebuilt in the 12th century, the bulk of the fabric was pulled down in 1809. Surrounding the church are the scanty remains of a Roman fort.

Whitstable Castle. A touch of the exotic, unknown to many visitors who take in only the seaside attractions of Whitstable. The castle, dating from the 18th and 19th centuries, stands on the site of an earlier house. It was later purchased by the local council, who opened the gardens to the public in 1948.

Above: **Meopham.** A long village that straddles the A227 road to Gravesend, Meopham possesses a beautifully preserved wind-mill, seen here across the wide expanse of the village green. The mill was built in 1801, the weatherboarding of its upper stages painted black above a brick base.

Opposite Top: **Eynsford.** The village of Eynsford has won awards for being the best kept village in Kent. Most travellers see only the main street, but just off to the side can be seen the early Norman remains of a castle and also this picturesque view of the River Darent, showing the medieval bridge and ford

Opposite Bottom: **Bluebells near Newington.** A blaze of springtime colour. Bluebells thrive in chestnut woodland on the North Downs and are particularly stunning in the first few years after coppicing. This ancient form of woodland manage-ment, when trees are felled and regrown from the stumps, can still be found in many parts of the county.   (Mrs V. Harris)

Above: **Bethersden.** A rare sight indeed, this fine group of oast houses near Bethersden stand ivy-clad and semi-derelict, providing a most romantic picture. Many oasts have now been converted into private dwellings.

Opposite Top: **Beltring.** The massed cowls on the oasts at the Whitbread Hop Farm are an unforgettable sight. Still a working farm, it is also a fascinating museum depicting the changing agricultural scene in Kent.

Opposite Bottom Left: **Rainham.** An even rarer sight in these days of automation are these hop stringers, using stilts to reach the tops of the poles and thread the twine for the vines to climb.   (Mr W.G. Thomas)

Opposite Bottom Right: **West Farleigh.** The hop vines are about a quarter grown in this early summer view. By midsummer they will have reached the tops of the poles and by September have formed a rich, fruit-bearing canopy.

Chilham. The square at Chilham looks almost too perfect to be true, but all is authentic. Medieval and Tudor houses line two sides, with the church and entrance gates to the castle lining the other two sides to complete the picture. Considered by many to be the most picturesque village in Kent.

Charing. Down a short side road off the main street in Charing can be seen this charming group of medieval buildings. To the right of the view stands the parish church, with to the left the remains of the Archbishop's Palace. Most of the palace buildings now form part of a farm.

Above: **Royal Military Canal, Hythe.** Begun in 1803 as a line of defence against French invasion, the Royal Military Canal roughly follows the old coastline prior to the draining and silting up of Romney Marsh. Originally the banks would have been kept clear to allow cannons an uninterrupted field of view.

Opposite Top: **Brookland Church.** There are many fanciful stories about the origins of the detached bell tower at Brookland, but the truth is more prosaic. A heavy tower would probably have been unstable on this site, so instead the bells were housed in a cage arrangement on the ground, later covered over by the wooden spire we see today.

Opposite Bottom: **Near Rolvenden.** A pastoral scene on the edge of the Weald, near Rolvenden, the windmill is of the type known as a post mill. Considerably smaller than tower or smock mills, such as Cranbrook, the entire body of the mill pivoted on a central post to catch the wind.

Above: **Cobham.** The 'Leather Bottle Inn' at Cobham was a great favourite of Charles Dickens, though in his day most of the timbering was covered beneath a layer of plaster. There is much to see in the village, including the church, with its unique collection of brasses, and attached priests' college.

Opposite Top: **Cooling Castle.** This view shows the splendid outer gatehouse of Cooling Castle (still privately owned) with its boldly projecting parapet. It was built in 1380 in response to the threat of invasion from France. The water has since receded to leave it stranded amidst lush marshland.

Opposite Bottom: **Otford.** Situated very close to the growing suburbs of Sevenoaks, Otford still preserves the essential character of a village with houses gathered around its pond and green. Just beyond are to be seen the gaunt remains of the Archbishop's Palace, built in brick about 1510.

Above: **West Malling.** Manor Park Country Park near West Malling High Street is magnificent, with many walks around the lake and across adjoining countryside. A road now separates the park, which is accessible, from Doucé's Manor, which is private. Nearby stand the ruins of a Norman keep.

Opposite Top: **Sutton Valence.** Where the crest of the North Downs sweeps down into the Weald can be found a number of hill-top villages. The main settlement, like this one at Sutton Valence, lies off to the side, parallel to the ridge and away from the through road, leaving the village largely unspoilt.

Opposite Bottom: **Loose.** The village of Loose, on the outskirts of Maidstone, is pure delight. The houses are built on the sides of a steep valley and everywhere can be heard the sound of running water. A number of streams flow through the village, which is more reminiscent of Devon than of Kent.

Left: **Goudhurst.** This view of Goudhurst was taken from the churchyard, which stands at the top of a hill at one end of the main street. There are many fine houses to be seen, a testament to the prosperity of the area over the years.

Below: **Bedgebury Pinetum.** This late summer scene at Bedgebury National Pinetum, near Goudhurst, shows the wonderful variety of foliage to perfection. The pinetum has the largest collection of conifers in Europe.

(Mrs V. Harris)

Opposite: **Scotney Castle Gardens.** Justly claimed by many to be the most romantic gardens in England, the castle at Scotney (1378), serves almost in the role of a picturesque folly, adorned with climbing roses and shrubs. (Eric Baldock)

Broadstairs. Probably the most attractive and least spoilt of all Kent's seaside resorts, Broadstairs has great charm. The town still preserves the character of a small fishing village and was much loved by Charles Dickens, who stayed at the house on the cliffs to the right, now known as 'Bleak House'.

Kingsgate. This delightful stretch of cliff-top walk passes Kingsgate Castle. Not a true castle, but one of a number of follies, built originally by Lord Holland in the 18th century. It is pure fancy and forms the perfect backdrop to Kingsgate Bay, below, with its beach of fine sand.

Above: **Aylesford Priory.** The first Carmelite priory to be founded in England was at Aylesford in 1242. Following the Reformation the monastery was converted into a private house. In 1949 the Carmelite Order bought the house and so returned to their former home, converting it back into a monastery.

Opposite Top: **Aylesford.** The view seen here of Aylesford village is perhaps one of the most photographed scenes in Kent, but it never fails to please. The bridge was built about 1370, though the central arch was widened in the early 19th century to ease the passage of river traffic.   (Tom Fowler)

Opposite Bottom: **The Countless Stones.** Little Kits Coty (known locally as the Countless Stones) is a ruined Neolithic chambered tomb. Legend says it is impossible to count the stones twice in succession and arrive at the same answer. The bright yellow crop in the field beyond is oilseed rape, an increasingly familiar sight in Kent.

Above: **East Farleigh.** This view of the River Medway at East Farleigh shows the magnificent medieval bridge, one of a number to be seen on this stretch of the river. The village straggles the hillside above the river and was once the home of Donald Maxwell, the noted Kentish historian and artist.

Opposite Top: **Teynham Church.** Seen here through the dappled sunlight of an early summer morning, Teynham Church now stands some way from the village proper. The first cherry orchards in England were planted at Teynham in Henry VIII's reign, though isolated cherry trees had been grown since Roman times.

Opposite Bottom: **Orchards at Norton.** Apple orchards, such as these at Norton, are still a fairly common sight in Kent. However, modern trees, while still providing a wonderful display of blossom in the spring, are much smaller, making fruit picking easier. (Miss F.A. Cheeseman)

Above: **Sissinghurst Castle Gardens.** Not a true castle, but a vast Elizabethan mansion, Sissinghurst is famed world-wide for the splendour of its gardens. The remains of the house, which was largely pulled down in 1800, forms a perfect backdrop to the gardens, laid out by Vita Sackville-West from 1930 on. (Mrs V. Harris)

Opposite Top: **Ightham Mote.** Another architectural gem, Ightham Mote is one of the best preserved moated manor houses in the country. The word *mote* originally meant a mound used as a meeting place. Later, the word was applied to the water-filled ditches that often surround such mounds. (Mrs V. Harris)

Opposite Bottom: **Hever Castle.** The magnificent gardens at Hever are largely the work of one man, William Waldorf Astor. He purchased the castle in 1903 and created what was to become one of the show places of Europe, including a lake, maze and statuary collected from around the world, especially Italy. (Mrs H. Thomas)

Lympne. There is much to see in this view, taken from what was once the sea bed before Romney Marsh was drained. To the right stand Lympne church and castle on what used to be the old cliff line. To the left, scattered down the hillside, are the tumbled remains of Stutfall, a Roman fort.

The Leas, Folkestone. There are two very distinctive sides to Folkestone. The old town and harbour are very much a typical family seaside resort. On top of the cliffs, however, all is different with sedate, tree-lined streets and gracious buildings. This view, looking towards the harbour, shows the delightful zig-zag cliff path.

Above: **Teston.** Another riverside settlement on the Medway that boasts a beautiful medieval bridge. A country park has been established on the river banks, which are particularly attractive here. Nearby can be seen a lock and weir, which whip the normally quiet waters into a racing torrent.

Opposite Top: **Allington Castle.** Just two miles from Maidstone stands the delightful Allington Castle. Built in 1282, by the early years of this century it had become a sadly neglected ruin. It was acquired in 1905 by Sir Martin Conway, who restored the ancient fabric to its former glory.

(Tom Fowler)

Opposite Bottom: **Headcorn.** This is another of those villages that has grown almost to the status of small town, but has somehow managed to retain its essential character. Headcorn boasts a wealth of timbered houses, such as the typical Wealden house seen here, right on the main street.

Above: **Bredgar.** Almost a suburb of Sittingbourne, Bredgar still preserves its village centre, which retains some fine old houses. Shielded from view, behind the trees to the right of the pond, stand the remains of a priests college.

Opposite Top: **Newington.** An evocative view of Newington church, seen across orchards and beneath a cloud-scudded sky. When the trees are in full bloom the church seems to float, like a stone galleon, on a sea of blossom. The area is still an important centre for fruit growing.

Opposite Bottom: **Lower Halstow.** The creek at Lower Halstow is one of many that punctuate the Medway estuary. Sailing barges, like the one seen here, were once a common sight on the river, but are now a rarity. There are some wonderful riverside walks to be had in the nearby marshes.

(Miss F.A. Cheeseman)

Above: **The Lighthouse, Dungeness.** The lighthouse shown in this view, built in 1960 to replace an earlier structure (which still stands a little way off), stands out starkly against the flat, lunar-like landscape. Dungeness is a unique and strangely haunting place, beautiful in its own way.

Opposite Top: **Dungeness.** The shingle at Dungeness is said to grow by several feet every year. The lakes seen here are the result of abandoned extraction workings. Nearby can be seen the grim buildings of the nuclear power stations alongside a nature reserve; truly an evocative place.

Opposite Bottom: **Old Romney.** Formerly a prosperous town, Old Romney has shrunk to the status of small village. When its harbour began to silt up in the Middle Ages a new settlement, New Romney, was founded nearer the sea, but that town too, like its older neighbour, is now stranded some miles inland.

Above: **The Guildhall, Faversham.** Faversham is another of those surprising places that boasts a wealth of historic buildings. The Guildhall, seen here, was built originally in 1574. The unusual oak pillars remain, though the rest was rebuilt in Victorian times. A market is still held beneath the arches.

Opposite Top: **The Creek, Faversham.** Situated on a creek leading to the Swale, Faversham has always had maritime associations. Ship building was for many years a major local industry, though sadly it has declined in recent years. The creek, however, remains a busy, working part of the town.

Opposite Bottom: **Davington.** On the outskirts of Faversham can be seen the charming village of Davington, overlooking an extensive pond. Davington Priory, on the hill behind, is a prominent feature. The abbey church now serves as the parish church, while the monastic buildings have been converted into a private residence.

Cranbrook. The Union Mill at Cranbrook, seen here standing high above the houses and shops of Stone Street, is a well-known local landmark. There is much weather-boarding to be seen in the town, including the upper stages of the mill itself. The windmill was built in 1814 and is open to the public at certain times.

54

Eastwell Park, Ashford. This highly picturesque entrance gate and wall are all that remains of a once great house, built about 1843 in Jacobean style. The original house has sadly been demolished. Standing forlornly within the park, and accessible by public footpath, are the bomb-shattered remains of Eastwell church.

Above: **Herne Bay.** An unusual view of Herne Bay, away from the hustle and bustle of the seafront so familiar to many summer visitors. This photograph shows the boating lake in Memorial Park, which lies only a short walk behind the High Street but could be in the middle of the countryside.

Opposite Top: **Lenham.** The square at Lenham is like a larger version of that to be seen at Chilham, slightly less perfect perhaps but none-the-less attractive. A car park occupies the centre of the square, where once a market was held, but lining the four sides are many fine old buildings.

Opposite Bottom: **Wickhambreaux.** Situated on the River Little Stour, the white weather-boarded watermill at Wickhambreaux makes a splendid sight. It stands as sentinel to the village, happily by-passed by two major roads, leaving it to slumber undisturbed amidst the lush countryside hereabouts.

(Mrs H. Thomas)

Above: **Offham.** This view of the green at Offham shows the only surviving quintain in the country, though it has been much renewed over the years. It was a device used to train horsemen in the art of using a lance in the Middle Ages. The large stone to the right is a mounting block.

Opposite Top: **Dover Castle.** This fine view shows perfectly the castle's impressive array of defences. Between the fields and the castle walls is a massive dry ditch. To the left of the view are the Saxon church, Roman lighthouse and Iron Age earthworks, all to be seen within the grounds.

Opposite Bottom: **Constable's Gate, Dover Castle.** The castle at Dover is one of the premier castles in England and in an excellent state of preservation. The impressive Constable's Gate was built between 1221 and 1227 and provides a suitably impressive entrance to this magnificent stronghold.

Wye. The River Stour, as it flows through Wye, has a sylvan beauty. Wye itself has grown to the status of small town, largely because of the presence of the Agricultural College of the University of London. It still retains the quiet peace of a village, however, and preserves many fine old houses.

St Margaret's at Cliffe. The chalk cliffs at St Margaret's are as high and equally as spectacular as those at nearby Dover. Most of the village occupies ground on the cliff-top, but a steeply winding road leads down to a delightful bay. Hemmed in by the cliffs, it is one of the least spoilt parts of the Kentish coast.

Above: **Smarden.** This charming view of Smarden shows the backs of cottages as seen from the churchyard. There are many timbered houses in the village, which many claim to have more houses of medieval date than any other settlement of comparable size in the country.

(Mrs V. Harris)

Opposite Top: **Minster, Isle of Sheppey.** The Abbey gatehouse and church at Minster are virtually all that remain of this once extensive monastery. The church is now used as the parish church, while the gatehouse, recently restored, houses a local history museum. There are uninterrupted views of the island from the top.

Opposite Bottom: **Kingsferry Bridge.** The stretch of water dividing mainland Kent from the Isle of Sheppey, the Swale, was for long crossed only by ferry. The present lift bridge, shown looking across marshland from the mainland side, was opened in 1960 and replaced an earlier bridge.

Sheerness. The North Kent coast is famed for the splendour of its sunsets, especially over the Swale. This evocative view, taken from the seawall at Queenborough, is spectacular and typical of the area.

(Mick Thomas)